IMAGES
of Wales

GOWER
PENINSULA

In 1924 the Gower Pageant was held at Penrice Park. Each village in Gower contributed an enacted scene from Gower's history. Here two girls from Llanrhidian pose in their costumes, being serving girls in *The Arrival of Lady Katherine Gordon at Weobley*.

IMAGES
of Wales

GOWER
PENINSULA

David Gwynn

TEMPUS

First published 2002
Copyright © David Gwynn 2002

Tempus Publishing Limited
The Mill, Brimscombe Port,
Stroud, Gloucestershire, GL5 2QG

ISBN 0 7524 2615 X

Typesetting and origination by
Tempus Publishing Limited
Printed in Great Britain by
Midway Colour Print, Wiltshire

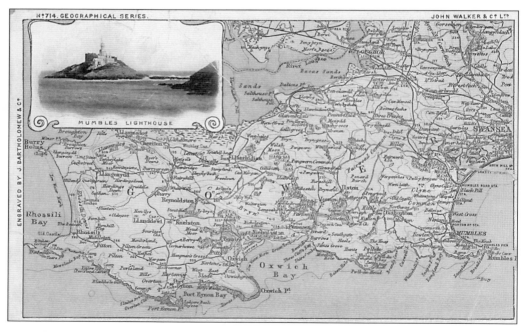

Map of Gower, *c.* 1908.

Contents

Acknowledgements

I would like to thank the following people, who have been kind enough to lend me photographs for inclusion in this book: Sandra Davis, Lawrence Oliver, David and Angela Nicholas, David Cowley, Roland and Linda Pritchard, H.D. Windsor Williams, John Owen, Sandra Jones, Philip and Denise John, Jennifer Griffiths and the late Barbara John.

I would like to dedicate this book to my wife, Alicia, without whose support it would not have been completed.

The first motor lorry to operate in Gower was owned by G.I. Thomas of Llanrhidian. This photograph was probably taken before the First World War, although the exact date is not known. The firm is still in business in Llanrhidian.

Introduction

The Gower Peninsula lies to the west of Swansea and is bounded by the Bristol Channel to the south and the Burry Estuary to the north. The first designated Area of Outstanding Natural Beauty, the peninsula is a place of small picturesque villages, dramatic cliffs, peaceful coves, patchwork farmland and wild, open moor. Its very diversity gives it a charm and character felt by many to be unique.

Throughout Gower can be found the evidence of a rich and varied history. Neolithic burial chambers, Viking names, Norman castles and churches, Georgian houses, mills, chapels – the list could go on. Gower has had an interesting history. There was industry – limestone quarrying along the south coast and cockle gathering at Penclawdd, along with coal-mining, tinplate and copper works. Agriculture, however, was and indeed still is the mainstay of the Gower economy, although today tourism is close to taking the crown as the top earner for the peninsula.

Gower has been a tourist destination for more than a hundred years and this has left a rich legacy of postcards, especially from the early years of the twentieth century, the so-called Golden Age of picture postcards. Many of the illustrations I have included are from postcards, many of which were locally produced cards by local photographers. Foremost amongst these was probably M.A. Clare of Mumbles, who seemed to have taken photographs of just about every corner of Gower, and every event in the early years of the century.

I have also been fortunate in being able to borrow a wide range of photographs, most of which have never been published before. The resultant mix will, I hope, give locals and visitors alike a sense of the old Gower, of the continuity still evident in the present-day communities, and of the people who live and work in Gower.

The publication of these photographs and postcards has only been possible because they were kept and treasured. Old photographs and postcards should never be destroyed. They are links with the past, windows into an age that cannot be recaptured. If anyone reading this comes into possession of old photographs or postcards of Gower that they wish to destroy – please don't – write to me care of the publishers. A good home will be found for them!

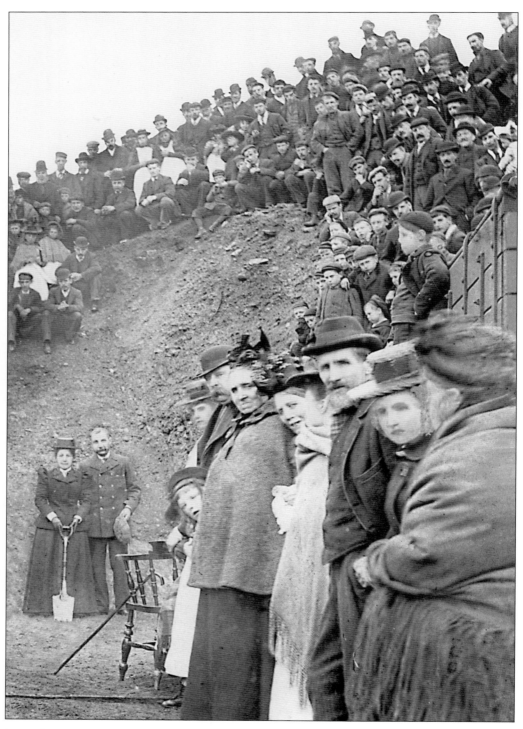

Mr and Mrs George Edward Gordon cutting the first sod at Penlan Colliery, Penclawdd, 1898. The ceremonial spade had a silver blade and an ebony handle.

One
The North Coast

Three Crosses sewing class, 1915. This photograph was probably taken outside Three Crosses School.

Llanyrnewydd church, c. 1915. The present church was built in 1850, but stands on the site of a chapel dating as far back as the sixteenth century.

A general view of Penclawdd from above Banc Bach, c. 1930. Notice that the view across the Burry Estuary shows the tinplate works of Llanelli.

A general view of Penclawdd, *c*. 1950.

Cockle gatherers at Penclawdd, *c*. 1900.

Mrs Margaret Phillips, Cwm Cynnar, selling cockles in Swansea Market in the 1930s.

Cockle gatherers leaving the marsh in the 1960s. Later the ponies and carts were phased out in favour of motorized transport.

Threshing at Rhian-Fawr Farm, above Penclawdd in the 1930s. By threshing, the grain would be separated from the stalks, before it was bagged up to be taken to a mill for grinding into flour.

The Camp, West End, c. 1950. These huts were erected as an army camp during the Second World War, and were then occupied by families in the post-war years. The Graig-y-Coed estate now stands on the plot.

Penclawdd County School RFC, season 1919/20. Unfortunately, the original photograph has suffered some damage, but its rarity warrants inclusion here.

This photograph of a Gower farming family was taken during the First World War at, it is believed, Penllwynrobert Farm.

Penclawdd Poultry Society, c. 1963. From left to right, back row, standing: Rowan Guy, 'Don' Williams, Emrys Matthews, Haydn Davies, William Guy, Robert John Davies, Elwyn Thomas, Ronald Tucker. Front row, sitting: Griff Lewis (secretary), Lewis Austin (treasurer). Front row, standing: Paul Tucker, David Tucker.

Passengers alight at Llanmorlais station in 1957. The branch line from Gowerton to Penclawdd was built by the Llanelly Railway and Dock Company in 1868. The LNWR took it over in 1873 and extended it to Llanmorlais. It was operated by the LMS after grouping in 1922, closed in 1957 and the track was lifted in 1959.

Unloading coal from a goods train in the siding at Llanmorlais station, 2 August 1957. This photograph gives a good view of the tiny station building.

Hawthorn Stores – which was much better known as 'Auntie Corrie's Shop' – Station Road, Llanmorlais, during the 1920s.

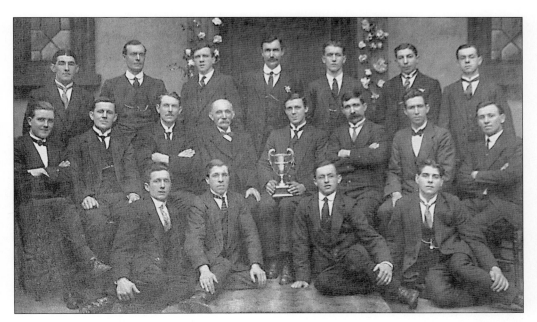

Quoits were played extensively in Gower, with many villages having a team. Here Crofty Light Quoits Club show off the Mr J. Williams MP Challenge Cup, which they won in 1919. From left to right, back row: W. Williams, W. Tanner, D.G. Hughes, D. Thomas, W. Jones, T.J. Thomas, T. Hughes. Middle row: T.J. Eynon, E. Williams, T. Guy, W. Bennett, J. Bennett, D. Hopkins, J. Hopkins, J. Harry. Front row: D.J. Hughes, A.L. Hughes, W.J. Hughes, A. Guy.

The miners of the New Lynch Colliery, Llanmorlais in 1914. This was the westernmost colliery in Gower at that time, and the seams went out under the Burry Estuary, so at times the miners could hear the water above their heads.

Llanrhidian village from the air, c. 1960. This view is of the bottom of the village.

Llanrhidian village from the air, *c*. 1980. Although this image is of the top of the village, comparison with the previous photograph highlights the amount of development undergone by the village in the intervening twenty years.

Two Italian prisoners of war laying a footpath in Llanrhidian, *c.* 1945. It seems that Italian prisoners of war were allocated to farms in Gower as extra labour just as the Second World War came to an end, and in the immediate post-war years. During the hard winter of 1946-47 Italian prisoners of war were used to clear snow from blocked roads in Gower.

The Green, Llanrhidian, *c.* 1912. The post office is on the right of the picture, and the large white building in the centre is the Welcome to Town Inn.

The post office moved across the road in the 1930s, as this postcard shows.

This general 1930s view of the village comes from the same series of postcards as the one above.

This view shows the old school, which is now the site of the church hall.

The present school, again from the 1930s series of postcards. It has been much extended and modernized in the intervening years.

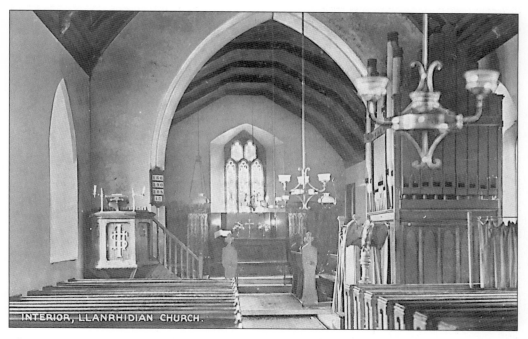

The interior of St Rhidian's church, Llanrhidian, 1930s. The present building is largely of thirteenth-century origin.

Woodlands, Llanrhidian. The group of buildings in the middle distance, on the edge of the marsh, is Stavel Hagar, an important centre of the Gower woollen industry in the nineteenth century.

Oldwalls, *c.* 1913. The chapel on the left-hand side of the road is Ebenezer, built in 1852 by the Calvinistic Methodists.

Caeforgan, Llanrhidian, from the air, *c.* 1965. Most of the outbuildings have now been converted into homes.

The youth hostel at Rosemead, Cilibion in its early days, *c.* 1950. The corrugated iron-roofed building nearest to the camera was the guests' kitchen until modernization took place.

An unusual form of transport used by hostellers in the early days.

The new dormitories at the youth hostel, which were built in the early 1960s.

Cutting timber at the Cilibion sawmills in the 1930s.

William Harry and a helper making a pitching pole at Cilibion Farm, probably in the late 1930s.

Skating on a frozen Broad Pool during the winter of 1960-61 (copyright *South Wales Evening Post*).

Cyril Sparkes with his cattle at Leason in 1968. Just north of Leason, out on the marsh, is the reputed graveyard of the *Scanderoon Galley*, a ship that was carrying chests of gold when it sank.

The Brandy House, Landimore, 1976. The original Brandy House was built at the end of the eighteenth century, it is said, specifically for smuggling, as it had a capacious cellar for hiding contraband.

Two
The Western Villages

CENERAL VIEW FROM CHERITON

A general view of Llanmadoc taken from the hill above Cheriton. In the foreground is the forge, with the Britannia Inn below it.

This 1950s photograph shows the forge as seen from the Britannia Inn. The line of the road to Ryers Down can be seen running up the hill behind the forge.

Mr Les Arnold, publican at the Britannia Inn, Llanmadoc, shown with some of his customers in the 1950s.

The Free Library, Llanmadoc, *c.* 1912.

The church of St Madoc, Llanmadoc, *c.* 1910. This is the smallest church in Gower, and is well known for the altar rails carved by the Revd J.D. Davies, a former incumbent of the parish and noted local historian.

Before motor buses arrived in Gower in 1909, horse-drawn buses carried passengers from the villages of Gower into Swansea. Here, the *Favourite* horse bus is shown setting out from Llanmadoc in around 1905.

A view of Cwm Ivy, *c*. 1930.

Llanmadoc celebrates the Coronation of Queen Elizabeth II in 1953, in a field opposite the Farmers Arms. This field was regularly used for the annual village sports day and other community events.

Whitford Lighthouse, *c.* 1930. This was built in 1865, entirely of cast iron, and ceased operating in 1933.

A view of Tulk Corner, Broughton Bay, Llangennith, c. 1920. Broughton Bay and Whitford Sands witnessed the worst maritime disaster to occur on the coast of Gower. On the night of 22 January 1868 sixteen vessels out of a fleet of nineteen that had just left Llanelli were wrecked in a storm.

Burry Holmes, c. 1950. This islet at the northern end of Rhossilly Bay boasts remains of the earliest religious settlements in Gower. The nearby village of Llangennith was an important religious centre from the sixth century onwards.

Llangennith church, *c.* 1910. The importance of Llangennith as a religious centre is reflected in the size of its church – the largest in Gower. The solidly-built tower and thick walls provided good refuge for villagers during the troublesome Middle Ages.

The Welcome Inn, Llangennith, *c.* 1900. The legendary Gower folk singer Phil Tanner lived here for many years.

This view of Llangennith, taken in 1949, shows the churchyard lychgate.

The road to Hillend, c. 1950. Today Hillend has a large caravan park, and is a popular venue for surfers who use Rhossilly Bay for their sport.

Phil Tanner was the last person to officiate at a Gower bidding wedding. Another tradition at Gower weddings was the firing of guns over the heads of the bride and groom as they left the church, to drive away evil spirits. It is believed the last time that this happened was at Llangennith in 1980.

Along with many other communities throughout Britain, Llangennith celebrated the Queen's Silver Jubilee in 1977 with great gusto. The fun and games were held at Coity.

Another view of the Llangennith Silver Jubilee celebrations of 1977.

William George Eaton of Burry Green with his champion heifer at Gowerton 1935. In the background is the railway line with a coal truck belonging to the local colliery owners, the Glassbrook Brothers.

The King Arthur Hotel, Reynoldston, *c.* 1910. Note the horse-drawn trap and the early motor car.

The King Arthur Hotel took its name from King Arthur's Stone on Cefn Bryn. Legend has it that King Arthur felt a pebble in his boot when returning victorious from the Battle of Camlan, and threw it many miles, and that it grew where it landed. Historians, however, prefer to tell us that it is a Neolithic burial chamber.

This view of Reynoldston, *c.* 1935, is taken from Cefn Bryn and shows the red road over the hill to Cilibion. It was named thus because the hill is formed of red sandstone, and before it was tarmacked, the road showed as a dusty red line over the hill.

St George's church, Reynoldston, *c.* 1910.

This view of Reynoldston, *c*. 1910, shows the post office in the foreground. Until 1968 this was the main post office in Gower, where mail was sorted before being taken out by postmen on foot or bicycle, or latterly in a van, to the other villages.

The ladies of the Tycoch All Souls church Women's Club enjoy a social event at the King Arthur Hotel in 1964.

The back entrance to Stouthall, 1912.

This road is now the A4118 – the main road from Swansea to Porteynon – but in this 1912 view Stouthall Avenue is a quiet narrow lane.

Stouthall was one of Gower's largest houses, and was occupied by John and Catherine Lucas from its completion in 1793. John Lucas erected a folly, in the form of a stone circle, in the corner of Upper Park. This photograph shows those stones in 1976, but they have now disappeared as a result of vandalism in the winter of 1995-96.

This 1970 photograph shows the craft shop in what was the old brewery on the Lower Green, Reynoldston. It is now a private house.

The new Reynoldston fire station was opened on 31 July 1951. The volunteer firemen stand ready for inspection.

The opening ceremony for the fire station was carried out by the chairman of Glamorgan County Council, Revd W. Degwel Thomas JP, with Mrs Thomas. The alarm was pressed by Mrs Thomas to signal the official opening. The party was completed by the chairman of the County Fire Services Committee; the clerk to the County Council and the chief fire officer.

The fire engine gleams on the first day.

Other guests and fire officers watch proceedings, unaware perhaps, that they have an audience of village lads.

The former Mewslade corner shop and craft shop at Middleton, Rhossilly in 1970.

Mewslade Rocks, c. 1905. The cliffs that make up the south coast of Gower were quarried extensively during the eighteenth and nineteenth centuries for limestone, which was burned in limekilns to provide lime for agricultural use. There was also a thriving export trade across the Bristol Channel to Somerset and Devon.

Rhossilly post office was situated at Middleton, and in the 1930s and 1940s was run by William Williams and his wife Gladys. Here they pose outside the post office in the 1940s.

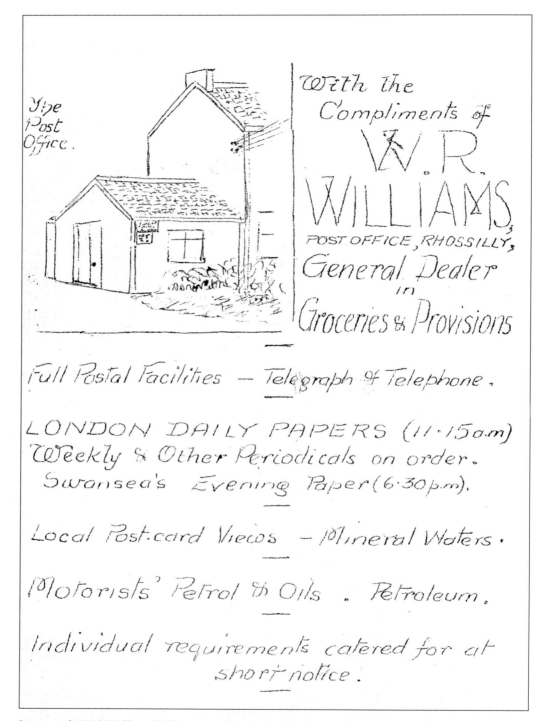

The Post Office.

With the Compliments of

W. R. WILLIAMS,

POST OFFICE, RHOSSILLY,

General Dealer

in

Groceries & Provisions

Full Postal Facilities — Telegraph & Telephone.

LONDON DAILY PAPERS (11·15a.m)
Weekly & Other Periodicals on order.
Swansea's Evening Paper (6·30p.m).

Local Post·card Views — Mineral Waters.

Motorists' Petrol & Oils . Petroleum.

Individual requirements catered for at short notice.

In around 1935 William Williams produced a leaflet for visitors advertising his services, which included a map of the area and details of bus services, church and chapel services etc. Reproduced here is the front page of the leaflet.

50

This photograph of Rhossilly post office was probably taken around 1930. Unfortunately it has suffered some staining.

The bonfire built on Rhossilly Down in 1935 to mark the Silver Jubilee of King George V.

John and Kathleen Pritchard making hay in 1955. They later moved from Rhossilly to Weobley Castle Farm, where Kathleen became custodian of Weobley Castle.

Jack Ace, Tom Pearce and John W. Owen at work on the coastguard lookout in Rhossilly, c. 1965.

St Mary's church, Rhossilly, *c.* 1935. A plaque in the church commemorates local man Petty Officer Edgar Evans RN, who perished with Captain Scott on his ill-fated Antarctic expedition in 1912.

Interior of St Mary's church, Rhossilly, *c.* 1910.

Being an exposed village, trees are rare in Rhossilly, and those that do grow have to adapt. This 1910 postcard shows an ash tree, partly sheltered by walls, that has grown horizontally.

Rhossilly village, *c.* 1910.

54

Rhossilly village viewed from Rhossilly Down, *c.* 1915.

Another view of Rhossilly from Rhossilly Down, *c.* 1935. Very little building work seems to have been carried out in the intervening twenty years.

RHOSILLy BAY.

This view shows the magnificent sweep of Rhossilly Bay and dates from around 1910. The buildings to the right of the picture, nestling under Rhossilly Down, are the old Rectory and its outbuildings.

WORMS HEAD COTTAGE RHOSSILLI

Worms Head Cottage, c. 1915. This subsequently became the Worms Head Hotel.

The children of Rhossilly school in 1966. The original photograph has suffered a little surface damage.

A school play being performed outdoors at Rhossilly school, probably in 1965.

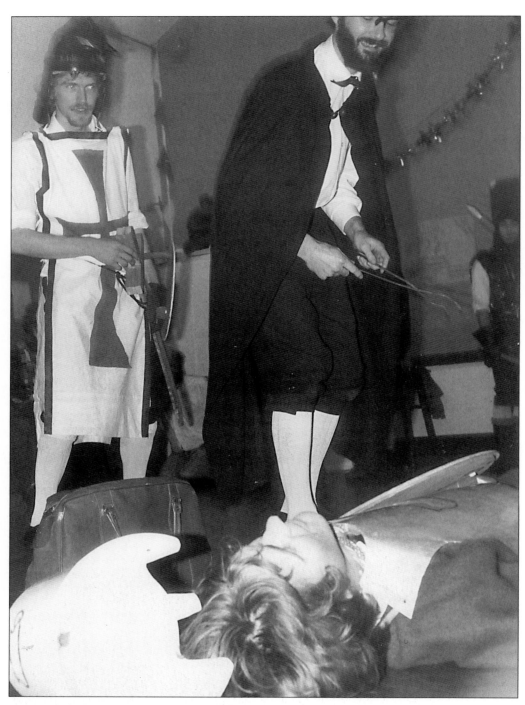

The Gower Mummers Play had been performed at Christmas time for centuries, and was commonly known as *The Christmas Sport*. It had, however, largely died out by the twentieth century. In the mid-1970s it was revived by the Men of Sweyn's Ey Morris Dancers. In this photograph, taken in 1978, the Doctor gets ready to cure the Turkish Knight who has just been killed by St George.

Three
The South Coast

Overton Mere, *c*. 1930.

Overton, *c.* 1920.

As a popular seaside destination for a hundred years or more, Porteynon is well represented by postcard views. This card shows Porteynon as seen from Overton in around 1910.

Of a similar date, this view looks up the village from what is now the car park on the seafront.

This early view, probably from around 1905, is taken from the churchyard.

This later view from around 1925 is taken from just a few yards nearer the road junction, and shows a clearer view of the lane leading to the beach. There have been only a few changes in the twenty years between these photographs. The shop sign on the left reads 'J. Jenkins, Grocer'.

Taken from above the church, this photograph gives a good view of the village. The lifeboat memorial can be clearly seen in the churchyard, so the view must date from after 1916, as that was the year of the lifeboat disaster.

This view looks up towards the churchyard and probably dates from the 1920s or early 1930s. It was published as a postcard by E.C. Grove of the post office, Porteynon, and may have been one in a packet of twelve, similar to that produced in Parkmill.

Taken from the sand dunes that separate the village from the beach, this view from 1905 shows Culver House on the right of the picture.

Not much has changed in this slightly later view of Culver House, although a new gate seems to have appeared in the extreme left of the photograph.

A lifeboat was stationed at Porteynon from 1884 to 1916. This postcard shows the lifeboat, *A Daughter's Offering*, which was in use between 1888 and 1909.

The Salt House, Porteynon, *c.* 1915. The Salt House was a fortified stronghold in the Tudor period, occupied by John Lucas, a member of the Lucas family of Stouthall, Reynoldston. John Lucas was a colourful character who tended to undertakings that were on the wrong side of the law. These ruins are of a much later cottage built on the site.

Repairing the sea defences near the Salt House, Porteynon in the 1960s. Jack Ace and John W. Owen appreciate some youthful assistance.

Sea defences were a necessary precaution at Porteynon, as this postcard of a stormy sea from 1915 shows.

Scouts and Guides enjoy some campfire entertainment at Porteynon in the 1930s.

The Scouts manage a dip in the sea. How the fashion in bathing costumes has changed! Today some beaches in Gower even see naturists soaking up the sun!

Camping at Porteynon in 1929. It is thought that most of these young men hailed from Penclawdd.

In this 1905 view Porteynon dominates the foreground, but in the background, the scattered houses of Horton can be seen.

The beach at Horton, *c.* 1920.

Gipsy Top, Horton, c. 1936. The beach huts have long since disappeared, as has a lot of the sand on Horton beach, due, it is feared, to excessive dredging for sand off the south Gower coast.

Horton Burrows, c. 1918.

Horton, *c*. 1930. The large house dominating the view is 'The Hollies'.

Horton, *c*. 1930, taken from the vicinity of 'Kiaworra'.

Cottages in Chapel Street, Horton, photographed in 1950.

Lulsley Hotel, Horton, *c.* 1930.

Slade Valley, *c.* 1907.

Slade Bay, *c.* 1910.

Oxwich Green, *c.* 1950.

Norton Farm, *c.* 1970.

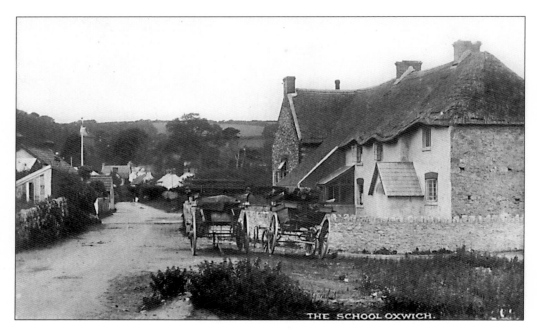

Oxwich School, *c.* 1919.

Pupils of Oxwich School, *c.* 1930.

Pupils of Oxwich School photographed on Oxwich Beach in around 1920. The close proximity of the beach and the sand dunes and marsh meant that nature rambles and nature study were always a large part of pupils' lessons.

The Cross area of Oxwich.

Wesley Cottage, *c.* 1905. This cottage was used by John Wesley on his visits to Oxwich.

General view of Oxwich with the marsh and dunes in the background, *c.* 1950.

A busy day on Oxwich beach, c. 1950.

A front view of Oxwich Rectory, c. 1945.

A side view of Oxwich Rectory, 1949. The Rectory later became Cliffside Guest House, and was then enlarged and modernized to become the Oxwich Bay Hotel.

Revd Canon Chastel de Boinville, Rector of Oxwich in the 1920s and 1930s, with his first wife and Dame Lilian Bayliss, the director of the Old Vic in London. Mrs Chastel de Boinville was a great believer in wholesome activities for girls, and ran dancing classes for them during the inter-war years. Dame Lilian was a noted benefactor of struggling artists and employed one to paint the chancel ceiling at Oxwich church.

Interior of St Illtyd's church, Oxwich, *c.* 1920.

Path up to Oxwich church, c. 1950. Up until the late eighteenth-century there were a number of houses beyond the church towards Oxwich Point. The gradual erosion of the land by the sea meant that these were abandoned and fell into the sea. The last to be abandoned was the old Rectory, leaving the church in a seemingly precarious position.

Revd S.W. Jenkins, Rector of Oxwich up until 1918. He was a much respected preacher who regularly drew large crowds to hear his sermons.

Oxwich Girl Guides pose by an ice cream van at Oxwich beach in around 1928.

Mrs Vera Clement and Mrs Minnie Jenkins pose outside 'The Bank', Oxwich, in around 1946. This photograph is interesting as in the background can be seen the white cottage known as 'Goosey'. This fell into disrepair soon after this photograph was taken and the ruin still stands on the site. A new 'Goosey' has been built in the garden.

Oxwich Tennis Club players pose
at the net in around 1937.

Oxwich Tennis Club.

Membership Card.

*Members may play any time during 19**40** Season
subject to the rules of the Club.*

W. A. Sainsbury,
Hon. Sec.

Oxwich Tennis Club membership card, 1940 season.

Oxwich Investiture celebrations, 1969.

Oxwich Silver Jubilee celebrations , 1977.

Mrs Wright, for a number of years the car park attendant at Oxwich car park, on Investiture Day in 1969.

Briar Dene, Oxwich in 1968.

View of Oxwich Marsh from Underhill, *c.* 1938, showing part of the walled gardens of Penrice Castle in the foreground.

The bottom of Oxwich Hill, *c.* 1935, showing Underhill Cottage, with the walled garden of Penrice Castle on the left-hand side.

Nicholaston Pill and Crawley Woods at the eastern end of Oxwich Bay, c. 1934. The Pill meanders out across the sands before reaching the sea, and has changed its course over the years, sometimes causing sand dunes to collapse beside it.

The village green, Penrice, c. 1936. Girl Guides again pose for the camera.

Another view of the village green at Penrice, this time showing the church, in around 1955. The white cottage on the right of the picture was called Sunset Cottage, and was attached to Rose Cottage. Sunset Cottage was demolished in the 1970s.

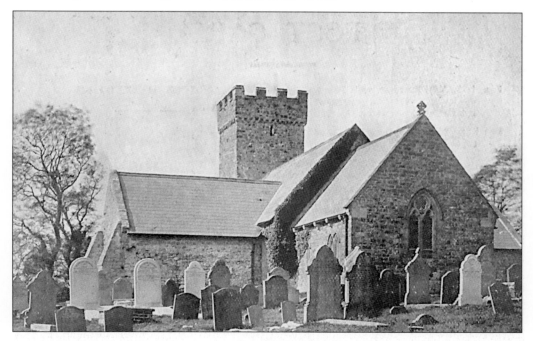

Penrice church, c. 1905. Dedicated to St Andrew, this Norman church contains signs that a Saxon mason had a hand in its construction.

Penrice Castle, c. 1910. This picture shows the original Georgian house with the lower, but probably larger, Victorian servants' wing, and a glass conservatory where the two parts of the house met. The Talbot family who owned Penrice also owned Margam Abbey at Port Talbot.

This 1930s view more clearly shows the extent of the Victorian addition, and it can also be seen that the conservatory has gone, replaced by a balcony. The entire Victorian addition has now gone, demolished in the late 1960s.

This 1910 postcard shows the house from the Norman castle which sits on a rocky escarpment above the Georgian house. The Norman castle is the most extensive castle in Gower.

This eighteenth-century engraving shows the ruins of the Norman castle, and the view across Oxwich Bay.

The ruins of the gatehouse of the Norman castle at Penrice, *c.* 1900.

The Talbot family were the biggest landowners in Gower. They employed a large number of staff at Penrice Castle. This photograph, taken in around 1902, shows the carpenters who worked on the estate.

Here one of the domestic staff at Penrice Castle poses for the camera in around 1904.

PENRICE. PARK
TREE PLANTED BY. KING EDWARD VII. 20 JULY 1904.

Tree planted at Penrice Park by King Edward VII on 20 July 1904. Various members of the Royal family visited Penrice over the years, with HRH The Prince of Wales (later King Edward VIII) being quite a frequent guest.

The Towers entrance to Penrice Park at the top of Oxwich Hill, *c.* 1905. The elderly female gatekeeper is shown attending as a horse and cart leave through the gates. This lady lived in the lodge which can be seen in the form of a tower on the left-hand side of the picture. This tower, the walls and another smaller tower just out of picture were really an eighteenth-century folly, rather than the genuine Norman remains they purport to be.

Gower Jubilee Fund

Garden Party

at

PENRICE CASTLE

to be opened by

His Grace The Duke of Beaufort K.G., P.C., G.C.V.O.

on

Saturday 2nd July 1977 at 3.00 p.m.

Music by West Glamorgan Youth Orchestra

Wine Bar
4.30 to 6.30 p.m.

Admission by Ticket Only: £2.50
(Strawberry tea included)

Invitation to the Gower Jubilee Fund garden party held at Penrice Castle on 2 July 1977.

Mr Christopher Methuen Campbell introduces the Duke of Beaufort at the garden party.

Again at the garden party, the cream of Gower society enjoy the beautiful sunshine and grounds of Penrice Castle.

The eighteenth-century granary at Penrice Home Farm. This building stands on mushroom-shaped supports in an effort to prevent vermin from entering and spoiling the grain. The photograph was taken in 1970, and a programme of restoration has been undertaken since then.

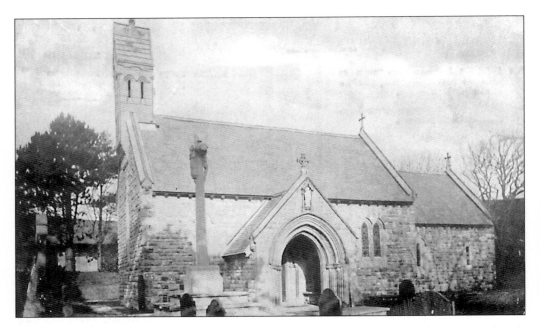

Nicholaston church, *c.* 1905. Dedicated to St Nicholas, this fourteenth-century church replaced an earlier church nearer the sea that had become besanded.

OXWICH BAY FROM CEFN-Y-BRYN, SOUTH WALES
60

A view of Oxwich Bay from Cefn Bryn with Nicholaston in the foreground, *c*. 1950.

Penmaen

A view of Penmaen with Three Cliffs Bay in the background, *c*. 1929.

Parry, Swansea

Three Cliffs Bay from Penmaen, *c.* 1904.

St John's church, Penmaen, *c.* 1905. This is also a fourteenth-century building erected to replace a besanded church on Penmaen Burrows. The besanded village on these burrows is thought to have been called Stedworlango.

The church and school, Penmaen, *c.* 1910.

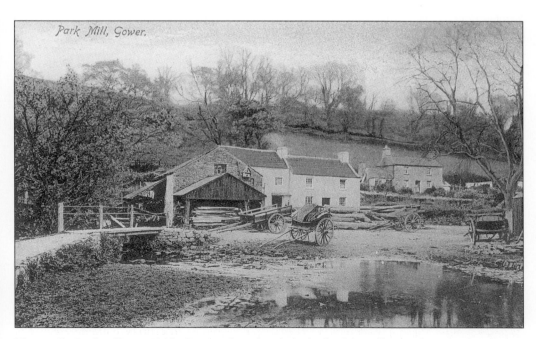

The mill, Parkmill, *c.* 1905. Restored and refurbished, the mill now houses the Gower Heritage Centre.

The western end of Parkmill, *c.* 1938. Shepherd's shop was a very small cabin at this time.

Shepherd's shop, Parkmill, *c.* 1960.

The police station, Parkmill, *c.* 1908.

Parkmill, *c.* 1905. There do seem to be a lot of schoolchildren in this photograph, but the school is prominent in the background, and a photographer in the village would have caused some excitement.

This view of the school was taken in around 1910, with the Gower Inn on the right-hand side.

The Gower Inn, photographed probably in 1912.

Broadwater Bridge, Parkmill, *c.* 1918.

The ruined chapel at Ilston Cwm, *c.* 1905. Built by John Myles in 1649, this was the first Baptist chapel in Wales. The threat of persecution during the Restoration period caused Myles to flee with some supporters to America.

The Baptist memorial at Ilston Cwm, *c*. 1930. This memorial was inaugurated by David Lloyd George in 1923.

Stones at Llethrid Cwm photographed in 1950.

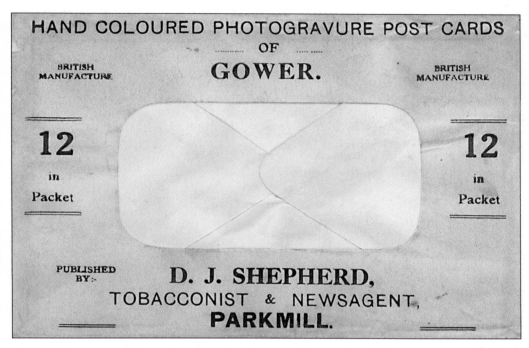

This envelope originally contained twelve postcards of Gower, published by D.J. Shepherd of Parkmill in the 1930s. Eight postcards remain in this particular envelope and they are reproduced as the next eight illustrations. Similar envelopes of postcards were probably published by other village shops in Gower, but they have not yet come to light.

Pennard Castle. Legend has it that the besanded village beneath the castle walls met its fate at the hands of angered fairy folk.

Three Cliffs Bay. Dangerous currents make this an unsafe place to bathe.

King Arthur's Stone. The flat piece was cut from the stone by a miller looking for a new millstone, but was then abandoned as suitable. This may have happened as early as the sixteenth century.

Oxwich Bay.

Ilston church.

Three Cliffs Bay and the Stepping Stones.

Pennard Castle.

Natural arch, Three Cliffs Bay.

The road near Kilvrough, *c.* 1905.

Kilvrough, *c.* 1910.

Kilvrough, *c.* 1910, showing the gardens.

The Folly, in the field known as Cocklebushes, Kilvrough, photographed in 1976.

Pennard church, *c.* 1905. This church, dedicated to St Mary, was built in the fifteenth century to replace the church lost when the village by the castle was besanded.

Pennard village, *c.* 1948. Today this area tends to be referred to as Southgate, 'Pennard' being used for the area around Pennard church around half a mile away.

Hunts Farm, Pennard, *c.* 1935.

Threshing at Hunts Farm in the 1930s.

Stacking the sheaves at Hunts Farm in the 1930s.

Posing at a delivery van, Hunts Farm, 1930s.

Highfield, Bishopston, *c.* 1910.

Bishopston Valley Hotel, *c.* 1905.

View of Bishopston church, with Kittle at the top of the hill on the opposite side of the valley. This photograph clearly shows the new road from Kittle to Bishopston and was probably taken in the 1930s.

General view of Bishopston, c. 1915.

Bishopston church with its ivy-clad tower, c. 1905.

Pyle Corner, Bishopston, *c.* 1935, with a camp in the background. Gibbs' shop is sheltered by the trees. The lane going past the camp leads to Brandy Cove.

View of Bishopston valley, taken in around 1940. In the eighteenth century the route up the valley from Pwlldu was used by the most successful smuggling gang to operate in Gower. The contraband was taken to the gang's headquarters at Great Highway and Little Highway farms.

Bishopston valley, photographed by M.A. Clare of Mumbles, *c.* 1910.

Pwlldu, showing Jenkins' Tea Rooms, *c.* 1900.

Pwlldu Bay, *c.* 1920.

In this photograph the 'Stewart Hall crowd' from Sketty enjoy a break at Jenkins' Tea Rooms, Pwlldu, in 1941. Several of those present were in the RAF, WAAF, WRNS or RN.

Brandy Cove, *c.* 1920.

The staff of Eastmoor Nursery, Clyne Common, 1948.

The official opening of Eastmoor Nursery, 1949. (Copyright *South Wales Evening Post*)

Caswell Bay, *c.* 1910. The boundary between the Gower Rural District and Swansea County Borough ran through Caswell Bay prior to 1974.

Four
Of Ships, Soldiers, and Shows.

Shipwrecks have been a feature of the Gower coastline through the centuries. Here the SS *Epidauro* lies at Washslade Bay, Overton, in February 1913.

The SS *Fellside* came ashore at Heatherslade Bay in January 1924.

The tug *Mumbles* on Oxwich Point, 1931.

122

The destroyer HMS *Cleveland* on Rhossilly beach in 1957. She was being towed to the breaker's yard when she broke free and ran aground.

The *Adherance* at Oxwich in the 1950s.

The *Ivanhoe* stranded at Horton in 1981.

William Williams of Rhossilly on horseback as a member of the Gower troop of the Glamorgan Imperial Yeomanry at their annual camp at Margam, 1908.

The Gower Troop of the Glamorgan Imperial Yeomanry on Sunday morning parade at the Newbridge-on-Wye camp in 1905.

WOMEN'S VOLUNTARY SERVICE FOR CIVIL DEFENCE

GOWER CENTRE

A STAND DOWN PARTY

will be held at

THE CHURCH HALL, REYNOLDSTON
ON TUESDAY, OCTOBER 23rd, 1945

to which you are cordially invited.

Address to be given by Miss D. GREEN, County Organiser

<u>TEA.</u>   MUSIC from 4.30 to 7.30 p.m.

An invitation to the Stand Down party of the Gower Centre of the WVS, October 1945.

The Gower Society was formed in 1948 to promote interest in Gower's history, wildlife and countryside. Here, the members meet for dinner in 1952. The tall gentleman seated at centre is Dr Gwent Jones, a driving force behind the fledgling society.

The Gower Show began in 1906 and has proved to be a lasting success and a major feature of the Gower calendar. In this photograph cattle are being made ready for judging at one of the 1930s shows.

Christie Pugh of Penrice receives an agricultural workers long service medal from HRH the Duke of Edinburgh at the Royal Welsh Show of 1975. (Copyright *South Wales Evening Post*)

Ploughing matches are held regularly in Gower. In 1953 the sixty-fourth Gower Union Ploughing match at Penmaen saw a young Trevor Beynon competing, with a little assistance from his father Tom. (Copyright *South Wales Evening Post*)

David Prosser competes in 1992.

Evan Evans, who taught at Llanrhidian school and was headmaster at Parkmill school was an accomplished photographer. This outstanding example of his work shows Walter Gwynn of Penrice outside the mill at Parkmill in 1960.